W9-AUL-689

HAIKU HARVEST

JAPANESE HAIKU
SERIES IV

TRANSLATION BY
PETER BEILENSON
AND HARRY BEHN

DECORATIONS BY
JEFF HILL

THE PETER
PAUPER PRESS
MOUNT VERNON · NEW YORK

FOREWORD

OF ALL the *haiku* I have read — in English, since I know hardly a word of Japanese — the three previous collections from Peter Beilenson's press, and his pen, in my opinion are the best, by far the best, translations. He brought each picture to instant life. He did not cloud nuance with words. And yet each poem is fully at home in our own language. Each has its own inner music, with the least alteration of content, no forced sentiment or emotion, no mere cleverness. Tenderness, irony, exuberance, vision, a listening, and always beauty — he sensed in each of these qualities a dialogue between this world and the world of the spirit, and he conveyed both image and echo.

Having so admired his three books of over six hundred *haiku*, when asked to complete his fourth, I was hesitant. I could only try to do what he would have done. Following his way of work, I read all the translations I could find, recited Henderson's phonetic Japanese versions for sound, absorbed Atasaro Miyamori's literal couplets and his sensitive notes, finally bursting out with what seemed the inevitable; what I felt the poet might have said in English.

In doing this job reverently in Peter's stead, I am grateful for the pleasant company of his friends, Basho, Buson, Issa, Shiki, and others of those old Haijin who spoke with such beautiful, evocative simplicity.

This should have been Peter Beilenson's book. He had just come to Basho's joyous shout about bringing a snowball in by the fire, when he died.

HARRY BEHN

HAIKU
HARVEST

JAPANESE HAIKU
SERIES IV

SNOW WHISPERING DOWN
ALL DAY LONG,
EARTH HAS VANISHED
LEAVING ONLY SKY

JOSO

DUSK, ADRIFT AT SEA . . .
WHY LOOK BACK
AT THOSE LESSER
HILLS HIDING FUJI?

KIKAKU

OH THAT SUMMER MOON!
IT MADE ME GO
WANDERING
ROUND THE POND ALL NIGHT

BASHO

CHANTING AND HUMMING
GONGS IMMERSE
THE GREEN VALLEY
IN COOL WAVES OF AIR

KYORAI

SO COLD ARE THE WAVES
   THE ROCKING GULL
    CAN SCARCELY
FOLD ITSELF TO SLEEP
BASHO

WHEN THE AUTUMN WIND
   SCATTERS PEONIES,
    A FEW
PETALS FALL IN PAIRS
BUSON

MY DEAR PILGRIM HAT,
   YOU MUST
    ACCOMPANY ME
TO VIEW THE PLUM TREES!
BASHO

HOW HOT AND DUSTY
   THESE SUNSTRUCK
    COBWEBS GLISTEN
BETWEEN DRY BRANCHES!
ONITSURA

TWICE PERHAPS THREE TIMES
   THE CHIMES OF THE RIVER
   CHANGED ...
OH WHAT A COLD NIGHT!
          ROKWA

EYES, YOU HAVE SEEN ALL ...
   COME BACK NOW,
   COME BACK TO THE WHITE
CHRYSANTHEMUM!
          ISSHO

A CUCKOO CALLS
   AND SUDDENLY ...
   THE BAMBOO GROVE
LIGHTED BY MOONBEAMS
          BASHO

ON THIS WELL-WORN STONE
   GARLANDED WITH
   PINKS OF SPRING ...
O TO DRINK AND DOZE!
          BASHO

HE WHO CLIMBS THIS HILL
   OF FLOWERS
    FINDS HERE A SHRINE
TO THE KIND GODDESS

          BASHO

MOONLIT FLOWER-FIELD...
   DAYLIGHT GIVES IT
    BACK AGAIN
TO A COTTON FARM

          BASHO

IF I COULD BUNDLE
   FUJI'S BREEZES
    BACK TO TOWN...
WHAT A SOUVENIR!

          BASHO

HAVING SPOKEN ILL
   MY LIPS NOW
    FEEL THE COLD OF
AUTUMN'S FATAL WIND

          BASHO

10

SOME POOR VILLAGES
   LACK FRESH FISH
   OR FLOWERS . . .
ALL CAN SHARE THIS MOON
               SAIKAKU

UNKNOWINGLY HE
   GUIDED US
   OVER PATHLESS HILLS
WITH WISPS OF HAY
              BASHO

UNCHANGED BY AUTUMN'S
   ICY WINDS . . .
   THE CHESTNUT'S SHELL
STAYS GLEAMING GREEN
              BASHO

MY EYES FOLLOWING
   UNTIL THE BIRD
   WAS LOST AT SEA
FOUND A SMALL ISLAND
              BASHO

THAT WINTER WHEN MY
FAITHLESS LOVER
LEFT ME ...
HOW COLD THE SNOW SEEMED
JAKUSHI

NO WONDER TODAY
ALL THE MEN NEED
MID-DAY NAPS ...
O THAT AUTUMN MOON!
TEITOKU

CHERRY BLOSSOMS, YES
THEY'RE BEAUTIFUL ...
BUT TONIGHT
DON'T MISS THE MOON!
SO-IN

AH THE FALLING SNOW ...
IMAGINE DANCING
BUTTERFLIES FLITTING
THROUGH THE FLAKES!
OEHARU

THIS OLD HAT, STOLEN
    FROM A SCARECROW...
    HOW FIERCELY
THE COLD RAIN PELTS IT!
                    KYOSHI

THE OAK TREE STANDS
    NOBLE ON THE HILL
    EVEN IN
CHERRY BLOSSOM TIME
                    BASHO

POPPY PETALS FALL
    SOFTLY QUIETLY
    CALMLY
WHEN THEY ARE READY
                    ETSUJIN

WHEN A NIGHTINGALE
    SANG OUT,
    THE SPARROW FLEW OFF
TO A FURTHER TREE
                    JURIN

THE STILL SNOW WE
   WATCHED ... HAS IT
   COVERED THE SAME HILL
AGAIN THIS WINTER?

           BASHO

UNDER A SPRING MIST,
   ICE AND WATER
   FORGETTING
THEIR OLD DIFFERENCE ...

           TEITOKU

IF MY GRUMBLING WIFE
   WERE STILL ALIVE
   I JUST MIGHT
ENJOY TONIGHT'S MOON

           ISSA

UNMOVED, THE MELONS
   DON'T SEEM TO RECALL
   ONE DROP
OF LAST NIGHT'S DOWNPOUR

           SODO

14

WHO CARES TO NOTICE
   CARROT FLOWERS,
   WHEN PLUM TREES
EXPLODE INTO BLOOM!

            SODO

DO THE TEA-PICKERS
   ALSO HIDDEN
   AMONG LEAVES
HEAR THE CUCKOO'S SONG?

            BASHO

IN MY SMALL VILLAGE
   EVEN THE FLIES
   AREN'T AFRAID
TO BITE A BIG MAN

            ISSA

OH THE FIRST SNOWFALL!
   WHO COULD STAY INDOORS
   ON SUCH
A GLORIOUS DAY!

            KIKAKU

IN STONY MOONLIGHT
   HILLS AND FIELDS
   ON EVERY SIDE
WHITE AND BALD AS EGGS . . .
          RANSETSU

WAKING BEFORE DAWN, SEE
   HOW THE CONSTELLATIONS
   ARE ALL
TURNED AROUND!
          RANSETSU

AMONG THESE LOVELY
   CHERRY BLOOMS,
   A WOODPECKER
HUNTS FOR A DEAD TREE
          JOSO

O THE TINY CRY
   OF A PITIFUL
   CRICKET
CAUGHT IN A HAWK'S BEAK!
          RANSETSU

EVEN IN CASTLES
    I HAVE FELT
        THE SEARCHING BREATH
OF THE WINTRY WIND
                    KYOROKU

EVEN I WHO HAVE
    NO LOVER ...
        I LOVE THIS TIME
OF NEW KIMONOS
                ONITSURA

CUCKOO, DID YOU CRY
    TO FRIGHTEN AWAY
        MY MOTHER
WATCHING IN MY DREAM?
                    KIKAKU

NOW THE DRAGONFLIES
    CEASE THEIR MAD
        GYRATIONS ...
A THIN CRESCENT MOON
                    KIKAKU

NEW YEAR DAWNING CLEAR...
　　CHEERFUL SPARROWS
　　CHATTER
ALL DAY LIKE PEOPLE
　　　　　　　　RANSETSU

PINE TREE SILHOUETTE
　　PAINTED BY THE
　　HARVEST MOON
ON A SHINING SKY
　　　　　　　　RANSETSU

WELL, THE FALL TYPHOON
　　HAS TAKEN
　　ITS FIRST VICTIM...
THE LOCAL SCARECROW
　　　　　　　　KYOROKU

A LEAF IS FALLING...
　　ALAS ALAS ANOTHER
　　AND ANOTHER
FALLS
　　　　　　　　RANSETSU

18

I'M VERY SORRY
    TO HAVE TO DIE
    AT THIS TIME
WITH PLUM TREES IN BLOOM
                    RAIZAN

HOW CAN A CREATURE
    BE SO HATED
    AS A WINTER FLY
YET LIVE SO LONG!
                    KIKAKU

POOR CRYING CRICKET
    PERHAPS
    YOUR LITTLE HUSBAND
WAS CAUGHT BY OUR CAT
                    KIKAKU

EVEN THE GENERAL
    TOOK OFF HIS ARMOR
    TO GAZE
AT OUR PEONIES
                    KIKAKU

19

EVERYTHING I TOUCH
  WITH TENDERNESS,
   ALAS
PRICKS LIKE A BRAMBLE
              ISSA

A YEAR HAS GONE BY
  AND STILL
   I'VE NOT YET LEARNED
MY NEW MASTER'S NAME
              RAIZAN

HELLO! LIGHT THE FIRE!
  I'LL BRING INSIDE
   A LOVELY
BRIGHT BALL OF SNOW!
              BASHO

A TRILL DESCENDING...
  BUT LOOK!
   THE SKYLARK WHO SINGS
THAT SONG HAS VANISHED
              AMPU

THINKING COMFORTABLE
    THOUGHTS
      WITH A FRIEND IN SILENCE
IN THE COOL EVENING . . .
           HYAKUCHI

THE SUN HAS GONE DOWN
    BEYOND A DEAD TREE
      CLUTCHING
AN OLD EAGLE'S NEST
           BONCHO

SNOW SETTLED TILL DAWN
    THEN CEASED . . .
      NOW SNOWFLAKES GLITTER
ON TWIGS IN THE GROVE
           ROKWA

WITH A WHISPERING HISS
    THE SCARECROW'S STRAW
      SCATTERS
AMONG THE STUBBLE
           BONCHO

21

AN OLD SILENT POND . . .
  INTO THE POND
    A FROG JUMPS,
SPLASH! SILENCE AGAIN
BASHO

I MUST GO
  BEGGING FOR WATER . . .
    MORNING-GLORIES
HAVE CAPTURED MY WELL
CHIYO

WHERE DOES HE WANDER
  I WONDER,
    MY LITTLE ONE,
HUNTING DRAGONFLIES?
CHIYO

COOL GREEN GRASS . . .
  ONE DREAM ALL HEROES
    FIND TO BE TRUE
ON FORGOTTEN TOMBS
BASHO

22

WANDERING, DREAMING,
　　IN FEVER
　　　DREAMING THAT DREAMS
FOREVER WANDER
　　　　　　　BASHO

THE SEED OF ALL SONG
　　IS THE FARMER'S
　　　BUSY HUM
AS HE PLANTS HIS RICE
　　　　　　　BASHO

AUTUMN CRICKETS CRY,
　　KOSAI THE POET
　　　IS DEAD,
HE NO LONGER SINGS
　　　　　　　KIKAKU

ANOTHER NEW YEAR
　　AND MANY ANOTHER
　　　FLEDGLING
WITHOUT A NEST...
　　　　　　　ISSA

HOW COOL THE GREEN HAY
   SMELLS, CARRIED IN
      THROUGH THE FARM GATE
AT SUNSHINE!

BONCHO

FAREWELL! LIKE A BEE
   RELUCTANT TO LEAVE
      THE SWEET DEEPS
OF A PEONY...

BASHO

HOME AGAIN!
   WHAT'S THIS?
      MY HESITANT CHERRY TREE
DECIDING TO BLOOM?

ISSA

THE DRAKE AND HIS WIFE
   PADDLING AMONG GREEN
      TUFTS OF GRASS
ARE PLAYING HOUSE

ISSA

24

WHEN SPRING IS GONE, NONE
   WILL SO GRUMPILY
   GRUMBLE
AS THESE CHIRPING FROGS
              YAYU

GAZING AT FALLING
   PETALS,
   A BABY ALMOST
LOOKS LIKE A BUDDHA
             KUBUTSU

MY HORSE CLIP-CLOPPING
   OVER A FIELD . . .
   OH HO!
I'M PART OF THE PICTURE!
             BASHO

HIGH ON A MOUNTAIN
   WE HEARD A SKYLARK
   SINGING FAINTLY
FAR BELOW . . .
             BASHO

25

BEYOND PAPER WALLS
  VOICES OF GEISHAS
  WHISPER
ABOUT THE BRIGHT MOON
            BASHO

THE STEAMING RIVER
  HAS WASHED THE HOT
  ROUND RED SUN
DOWN UNDER THE SEA
            BASHO

SWALLOWS! THOSE HOMING
  BEES IN THE SUNSET
  BURDENED WITH HONEY,
SPARE THEM!
            BASHO

OVER THE RUINS
  OF A SHRINE,
  A CHESTNUT TREE
STILL LIFTS ITS CANDLES
            BASHO

26

IT IS NICE TO READ
　　NEWS THAT OUR
　　SPRING RAIN ALSO
VISITED YOUR TOWN
　　　　　　ONITSURA

AT LAST, WHEN HER SONG
　　IS STILL
　　THE GODDESS BECOMES
A SMALL GREEN BIRD
　　　　　　ONITSURA

A WIND-BELL TINKLING,
　　HUSHED IN THE NOON SUN
　　IS NOW
A SHELTER FOR BEES
　　　　　　GONSUI

WHAT USE NOW ARE TWIGS
　　BUT TO SWEEP UP
　　A LITTER
OF FALLEN PETALS?
　　　　　　BUSON

27

IN A WAYSIDE SHRINE,
  A HUNGRY OWL
    HOOTS AND HIDES,
SO BRIGHT IS THE MOON!
JOSO

ABOVE THE PILGRIMS
  CHANTING
    ON A MISTY ROAD
WILD GEESE ARE FLYING
RANSETSU

ALL NIGHT THE RAGGED
  CLOUDS AND WIND
    HAD ONLY ONE
COMPANION . . . THE MOON
BONCHO

HOW STILL IT IS!
  CICADAS
    BUZZING IN SUN
DRILLING INTO ROCK . . .
BASHO

WE ROWED INTO FOG,
    AND OUT THROUGH FOG . . .
    O HOW BLUE
HOW BRIGHT THE WIDE SEA!
                    SHIKI

FROM WATCHING THE MOON
    I TURNED
    AND MY FRIENDLY OLD
SHADOW LED ME HOME
                    SHIKI

WHEN MY CANARY
    ESCAPED, WELL
    THAT WAS THE END
OF SPRING IN MY HOUSE
                    SHIKI

A VOICELESS FLOWER
    SPEAKS
    TO THE OBEDIENT
IN-LISTENING EAR
                    ONITSURA

29

WITHOUT MY HAT! BAH!
  WHY DOES THIS RAIN
    HAVE TO PLOP ON MY PATE!
OH, WELL!

               BASHO

BECAUSE SPRING HAS COME,
  THIS SMALL GRAY
    NAMELESS MOUNTAIN
IS HONORED BY MIST

               BASHO

WAKE UP! WAKE UP! COME
  SLEEPY BUTTERFLY
    PLEASE JOIN ME
ON MY JOURNEY!

               BASHO

LITTLE BIRD FLITTING,
  TWITTERING, TRYING
    TO FLY...
MY, AREN'T YOU BUSY!

               BASHO

30

A SMALL HUNGRY CHILD
   TOLD TO GRIND RICE,
   INSTEAD
GAZES ON MOONLIGHT
                 BASHO

WHAT BLOOM ON WHAT TREE
   YIELDS
   THIS IMPERCEPTIBLE
ESSENCE OF INCENSE?
                 BASHO

PATIENCE, FROST!
   AFTER THESE FEW
     THERE WILL BE NO MORE
WHITE CHRYSANTHEMUMS
                OEMARU

HOP OUT OF MY WAY
   AND ALLOW ME PLEASE
     TO PLANT BAMBOOS,
MR. TOAD!
             CHORA

31

WASHING MY RICE HOE,
RIPPLES FLOW AWAY...
AS UP
FLY THE PIPING SNIPE!

BUSON

SPRING IS NEARLY GONE
SO NOW
THIS OLD CHERRY TREE
DECIDES TO BLOOM!

BUSON

FLOWERS IN SHADOW...
A MOON FLOATING
IN THE EAST,
IN THE WEST, THE SUN

BUSON

DAY DARKEN! FROGS SAY
BY DAY... BRING LIGHT!
LIGHT! THEY CRY
BY NIGHT. OLD GRUMBLERS!

BUSON

32

TIDES OF THE SPRING SEA,
   TIDE AFTER INDOLENT TIDE
   DRIFTING
ON AND ON . . .
           BUSON

BEYOND THE TEMPLE
   AND THE GARDEN LANTERNS,
   SWANS
AFLOAT AND ASLEEP . . .
           SHIKI

AS SHE WASHES RICE,
   HER SMILING FACE
   IS BRIEFLY
LIT BY FIREFLY
           ANON.

A MOUNTAIN VILLAGE
   LOST IN SNOW . . .
   UNDER THE DRIFTS
A SOUND OF WATER
           SHIKI

ONE MAN AND ONE FLY
   BUZZING TOGETHER
   IN ONE BIG BARE
SUNNY ROOM ...

ISSA

WITHERED TUFTS OF GRASS ...
   ONCE UPON A TIME
   THERE WAS, AND IS,
AN OLD WITCH!

ISSA

SINCE I FIRST BECAME
   A HERMIT,
   THE FROGS HAVE SUNG
ONLY OF OLD AGE

ISSA

THERE GOES A BEGGAR
   NAKED
EXCEPT FOR HIS ROBES
OF HEAVEN AND EARTH!

KIKAKU

OLD MAN WITH ONE EAR
HELD CLOSE,
    DO I SOUND TO YOU
LIKE A BUZZING GNAT?
                    ISSA

A SNOWY MOUNTAIN
    ECHOES IN THE
    JEWELED EYES
OF A DRAGONFLY
                    ISSA

HEAVY WAVES CRASHING...
    SILENTLY
    OVER SADO
FLOWS HEAVEN'S RIVER
                    BASHO

THIS IS MY OWN SNOW
    THAT SAGS
    MY OLD MATTED HAT,
AND IT'S LIGHT AS DOWN!
                    KIKAKU

HAWKS OVER THE SEA...
　　AS WE
　　IN OUR VILLAGE DANCE
IN SMALLER CIRCLES
　　　　　　　　　TAIGI

WE COVER FRAGILE BONES
　　IN OUR FESTIVE BEST
　　TO VIEW
IMMORTAL FLOWERS
　　　　　　　　　ONITSURA

THE LEAVES NEVER KNOW
　　WHICH LEAF
　　WILL BE FIRST TO FALL...
DOES THE WIND KNOW?
　　　　　　　　　SOSEKI

MOON ADRIFT IN A CLOUD...
　　I HAVE A MIND
　　TO BORROW
A SMALL RIPE MELON
　　　　　　　　　SHIKI

36

PREACH AWAY, CRICKET,
    IT DOESN'T MATTER TO ME.
    I KNOW
IT'S AUTUMN
                        SOSEKI

I MIGHT FEEL COOLER
    IF I WERE THE
    EMPEROR OF ROCKS
IN THE SEA
                        SOSEKI

SINCE NO BELLS RESOUND
    IN THIS TOWN,
    WHAT DO PEOPLE DO
ON SPRING EVENINGS?
                        BASHO

UNDER THE TEMPLE EAVES
    GOLD FADES . . .
    THROUGH BUDDING LEAVES
WE LOOK TOWARD THE PAST
                        CHORA

37

WHOSE DRESS COULD THIS BE
   THIN ON THE LEAF-GOLD
   AUTUMN SCREEN?
ONLY THE WIND'S

          BUSON

ALL DAY IN GREY RAIN
   HOLLYHOCKS
   FOLLOW THE SUN'S
INVISIBLE ROAD

          BASHO

JEWELS OF SMALL SHELLS
   IN RIPPLES
   OF SAND, TANGLED
WITH KELP AND RUBBISH

          BASHO

AFTER BELLS HAD RUNG
   AND WERE SILENT...
   FLOWERS CHIMED
A PEAL OF FRAGRANCE

          BASHO

BROWN LEAF FROM A TREE
   UNKNOWN CLINGS
   TO A STRANGE
GREEN-SPOTTED MUSHROOM
           BASHO

LIGHTNING FLICKERING
   WITHOUT SOUND...
   HOW FAR AWAY
THE NIGHT-HERON CRIES!
           BASHO

OUT OF ONE WINTRY
   TWIG, ONE BUD,
   ONE BLOSSOM'S WORTH
OF WARMTH AT LONG LAST!
           RANSETSU

BEHIND ME THE MOON
   BRUSHES
   SHADOWS OF PINE TREES
LIGHTLY ON THE FLOOR
           KIKAKU

39

A NIGHT BRIGHT WITH STARS...
   WHOSE GHOST IS THIS
   WHISPERING:
SHALL I LIGHT THE LAMP?
                    ETSUJIN

RIPE HEADS OF BARLEY
   BENT DOWN BY A RAIN,
   BOWING
NARROW MY PATHWAY
                    JOSO

IT IS NOT EASY
   TO BE SURE WHICH END
   IS WHICH
OF A RESTING SNAIL
                    KYORAI

HO, FOR THE MAY RAINS!
   FROGS SWIM
   IN THROUGH MY OPEN
DOOR FOR A VISIT!
                    SANPU

40

AROUND THE GLOWING COALS
   OF A BRAZIER,
   OLD MEN TELL TALES
OF EARTHQUAKES
                    KYOROKU

OH HOW I ENJOY
   EATING A RIPE PERSIMMON
   WHILE DEEP
OLD BELLS BOOM!
                    SHIKI

FROG-SCHOOL COMPETING
   WITH LARK-SCHOOL
   SOFTLY AT DUSK
IN THE ART OF SONG...
                    SHIKI

ONE PERFECT MOON
   AND THE UNCOUNTABLE
   STARS
DROWNED IN A GREEN SKY
                    SHIKI

41

THE BEST I HAVE
  TO OFFER YOU
  IS THE SMALL SIZE
OF THE MOSQUITOES

BASHO

IF THINGS WERE BETTER
  FOR ME, FLIES,
  I'D INVITE YOU
TO SHARE MY SUPPER

ISSA

SLACK SAILS PUFFING FULL
  GLINT ON THE SEA
  IN A QUICK BRIGHT
WINTER SHOWER

KYORAI

UP FROM THE BOTTOM
  OF AN OLD POND,
  THAT DUCKLING
HAS SEEN SOMETHING STRANGE

JOSO

A THREE-DAY-OLD MOON
  ALREADY WARPED
  AND TWISTED
BY THE BITTER COLD!
                    ISSA

AT DAWN MY CASTLE
  WAS STORMED
  BY A FLIGHT OF DUCKS
QUACKING IN A MIST
                    KYOROKU

ONLY A CHIRPING
  INSECT TOLD ME
  IT WAS NIGHT,
SO BRIGHT WAS THE MOON
                    ETSUJIN

NOT UNTIL I'D LOOKED
  A LONG TIME
  AT THE NEW SNOW
DID I WASH MY FACE
                    ETSUJIN

SMALL BIRD FORGIVE ME,
   I'LL HEAR THE END
   OF YOUR SONG
IN SOME OTHER WORLD
                    ANON.

A RED LEAF FALLING,
   SETTLING
   INTO THE RIVER,
CLINGS TO A GREEN ROCK
                    JOSO

CALMLY FUJI STANDS
   HIGH ABOVE
   THE NEW LEAVES' WAVES
THAT BURY THE EARTH
                    BUSON

ON THE TEMPLE'S GREAT
   BRONZE BELL,
   A BUTTERFLY SLEEPS
IN THE NOON SUN
                    BUSON

WHAT A PRETTY KITE
   THE BEGGAR'S CHILDREN
   FLY HIGH
ABOVE THEIR HOVEL!
               ISSA

A CROW CLINGS SILENT
   TO A BARE BOUGH,
   CAUTIOUSLY
WATCHING THE SUNSET
               BASHO

HOW FAR THE SKYLARK SOARS
   OVER
   A CLOUD-MOUNTAIN
BREATHING-IN SUN-MIST!
               SHIKI

IN THIS TOWN
   WHERE I WAS BORN,
   TONIGHT MY ONLY FRIENDS
ARE THE CRICKETS
               ANON.

45

DEFTLY THE NEW MOON
   BRUSHES
   A SILVER HAIKU
ON THE TIPS OF WAVES
         KYOSHI

RAIN FALLING AT DUSK
   SWEPT ON, ON,
   SPILLING MILLIONS
OF MOONS ON GRASS-BLADES
         SHO-U

CHANTING A PRAYER,
   MY HEART IS TWINED
   IN GARLANDS
OF MORNING-GLORIES
         KYOROKU

SINCE MY HOUSE
   BURNED DOWN, I NOW OWN
   A BETTER VIEW
OF THE RISING MOON
         MASAHIDE

46

SCARECROWS ARE THE FIRST
   HEROES TO FALL
    IN THE RUSH
OF THE AUTUMN WIND
             KYOROKU

BEANS FROM VINES
   GROWING OVER A
    SCARECROW
ARE EASY TO STEAL
            YAYU

SHAKING HIS LOOSE SKIN,
   A TIRED OLD HORSE
    SCARES AWAY
A WHITE BUTTERFLY
            ISSA

WHERE ARE MY NEIGHBORS?
   WHY DO THEY SEEM
    SO QUIET
THIS AUTUMN EVENING?
            BASHO

47

UNDER A FULL MOON
   ON A DISTANT
   TIDELESS SHORE
I HEAR MEN SHOUTING
SHURIN

A POOL REFLECTING
   WHITE CLOUDS . . .
   DEEP IN A BAMBOO
SHADOW, A FISH STIRS
SHURIN

WHAT DOES THIS MEAN?
   CHRYSANTHEMUMS
   AND JONQUILS
BLOOMING TOGETHER!
SHURIN

BRIEFLY THE SUN SHINES
   BRIGHTLY BETWEEN
   CLOUD AND SEA
FADING AS RAIN FALLS
ONTEI

48

WHEN THE TIGHT STRING
    SNAPPED, THE KITE FELL
    FLUTTERING...THEN...
IT LOST ITS SPIRIT
                    KUBONTA

IDLY, A SHIP GLIDES,
    THE TIP OF ITS SAIL
    DIPPING
THE POLISHED WATER
                    OTSUJI

INTO A COLD NIGHT
    I SPOKE ALOUD...
    BUT THE VOICE WAS
NO VOICE I KNEW
                    OTSUJI

CAREFULLY PUTTING
    HIS GOLDFISH BOWL
    ON THE PATH
HE RAN TO A FIRE
                    GESSHU

49

A HORSEFLY BUZZES
   LOUD
     IN THE SHINING HOLLOW
OF A TEMPLE BELL

             BOKUSUI

OVER THE WINTRY FOREST,
   WINDS HOWL
     IN A RAGE
WITH NO LEAVES TO BLOW

             SOSEKI

CUCKOO, IF YOU MUST,
   CRY TO THE MOON,
     NOT TO ME . . .
I'VE HEARD YOUR STORY

             SOSEKI

BUTTERFLY! THESE WORDS
   FROM MY BRUSH
     ARE NOT FLOWERS . . .
ONLY THEIR SHADOWS

             SOSEKI

THE MIGHTIEST GODS
  LOOM NAKED
  IN A BLACK WIND
LAUGHING AT DEMONS
                    SOSEKI

A RAIN CLOUD DARKENS
  RED MAPLES
  CLINGING TO CRAGS
BY A WATERFALL
                    SOSEKI

THE RIVER LEAPING
  ROCKS, ANGRILY
  ROARS AWAY...
AS THE MOUNTAIN SMILES
                    MEISETSU

BROKEN AND BROKEN
  AGAIN ON THE SEA,
  THE MOON
SO EASILY MENDS
                    CHOSU

51

EACH ELEGANT TREE
   HAS ITS OWN NAME...
THIS BEAUTY,
THE NIGHTINGALE'S ROOST
SOSEKI

DREAMING OF SHOUTING
   CICADAS,
   I WAKEN PARCHED
FROM MY NOONDAY NAP
SOSEKI

HONKING WILD GEESE COME
   SCRAWLING DELIGHT
   IN SPRING'S COLD
PALE MORNING SUNLIGHT
SO-IN

BUTTERFLIES!
   BEWARE OF THE SHARP
   NEEDLES OF PINES
IN THIS GUSTY WIND!
SHUSEN

O MOON,
    WHY MUST YOU INSPIRE
    MY NEIGHBOR TO CHIRP
ALL NIGHT ON A FLUTE!
              KOYO

I KNEW FROM THE SOUND
    OF HIS TINKLING BELL
    A PRIEST WAS THERE
IN THE MIST
              MEISETSU

WATCHING THE SPRING MOON
    RISE,
    I NO LONGER BOTHER
ABOUT THE MOUNTAINS
              KYORAI

UNDER A HELMET
    HUNG IN A SHRINE,
    A CRICKET
CHIRPS HIS LAST COMMAND
              BASHO

I CALLED OUT: WHO'S THERE?
   WHOEVER IT WAS
   IN SNOW
STILL KNOCKS AT MY GATE
          KYORAI

BEYOND THE MOUNTAIN
   I WATCHED THE RAINBOW
   PAINTING
THE SAGE'S VISION
          MEISETSU

WHERE THE CUCKOO'S DARK
   SONG CROSSES
   THE SKYLARK'S CLEAR
HIGH SONG, THERE AM I!
          KYORAI

THE SPEECH OF INSECTS
   AND THE SPEECH OF MEN
   ARE HEARD
WITH DIFFERENT EARS
          SHIKI

A RED MOON GOES DOWN
LATE IN THE WEST...
SHADOWS FLOW EASTWARD
AND VANISH

BUSON

AFTER A SHOWER,
THE CLEARING SKY
SMELLS FAINTLY
OF HAWTHORNE BLOSSOMS

SHIKI

IN MY HOUSE THIS SPRING,
TRUE, THERE IS NOTHING,
THAT IS,
THERE IS EVERYTHING!

SODO

FOOLISH DUCKS,
YOU KNOW MY REEDY POND
IS OLD AND
WATCHED BY A WEASEL!

BUSON

55

WILD GEESE HAVE EATEN
ALL OF MY BARLEY...
ALAS,
THEY ARE FLYING ON!

YASUI

OVER THE DEEPEST
DARKEST RIVER,
THE FIREFLIES
ARE FLOWING SLOWLY

SHIYO

AS FROGLETS
THEY SANG LIKE BIRDS...
NOW SUMMER IS GONE
THEY BARK LIKE OLD DOGS

ONITSURA

THE SLIGHTEST BREEZE
BLOWS AND THE SKY'S DRY
SHELL IS FILLED
WITH THE VOICE OF PINES

ONITSURA

COME COME! I CALL.
   BUT THE FIREFLIES
     FLASH AWAY
INTO THE DARKNESS
           ONITSURA

WARBLER IN MY PLUM TREE,
   PERCHING THERE
     IS AN OLD
CUSTOM OF YOUR CLAN
           ONITSURA

EVEN STONES IN STREAMS
   OF MOUNTAIN WATER
     COMPOSE
SONGS TO WILD CHERRIES
           ONITSURA

AT LAST! IN SUNSHINE
   SPARROWS
     ARE BATHING IN SAND,
FLUFFING THEIR FEATHERS
           ONITSURA

A TREE FROG SOFTLY
   BEGINS TO TRILL
   AS RAIN DROPS
SPATTER THE NEW LEAVES
          ROGETSU

A DRIFT OF ASHES
   FROM A BURNED FIELD,
   A WAILING
WIND SIGHING AWAY...
          ONITSURA

WHAT A SPLENDID DAY!
   NO ONE IN ALL
   THE VILLAGE
DOING ANYTHING!
          SHIKI

WHY DO THEY WANDER
   OVER THE GREEN HILLS
   IN SPRING?
WHY DO THEY COME HOME?
          SHIKI

58

BEYOND A DARK WOOD
  LIGHTNING REVEALED
    STILL WATER,
BRIGHT, LIKE A VISION
                    SHIKI

IF THE WHITE HERONS
    HAD NO VOICE
      THEY WOULD BE LOST
IN THE MORNING SNOW
                    CHIYO

LEAF FALLING ON LEAF,
    ON PILED-UP LEAVES ...
      RAIN SPLASHING
IN POOLS OF RAIN ...
                    GYODAI

ENVIABLE LEAVES,
    BECOMING
      SO BEAUTIFUL
JUST BEFORE FALLING ...
                    SHIKI

LIGHTNING FLASHING
   ALL NIGHT IN THE EAST
   THIS MORNING
SMOULDERS IN THE WEST
              KIKAKU

THE ROOSTER, FIGHTING,
   SPREADING
   HIS RUFF OF FEATHERS,
THINKS HE'S A LION!
              KIKAKU

A BABY WARBLER GAILY
   SWINGING
   UPSIDE-DOWN
SINGS HIS FIRST SONG!
              KIKAKU

YOU FLEAS SEEM TO FIND
   THE NIGHT AS LONG
   AS I DO.
ARE YOU LONELY, TOO?
              ISSA

60

THE SEA THIS AUTUMN
    EVENING IS GREEN,
    THE RICE FIELD
IS GREEN AS THE SKY
                    BASHO

WELL! HELLO DOWN THERE,
    FRIEND SNAIL!
    WHEN DID YOU ARRIVE
IN SUCH A HURRY?
                    ISSA

AS MOUNTAIN SHADOWS
    DARKEN MY GATE,
    THE TEMPLE DEER
STILL SEE SUN-RAYS
                    BUSON

HE IS UNKNOWN,
    THE POET WHO SINGS
    THIS GREATEST
OF ALL SONGS — SPRING!
                    SHIKI